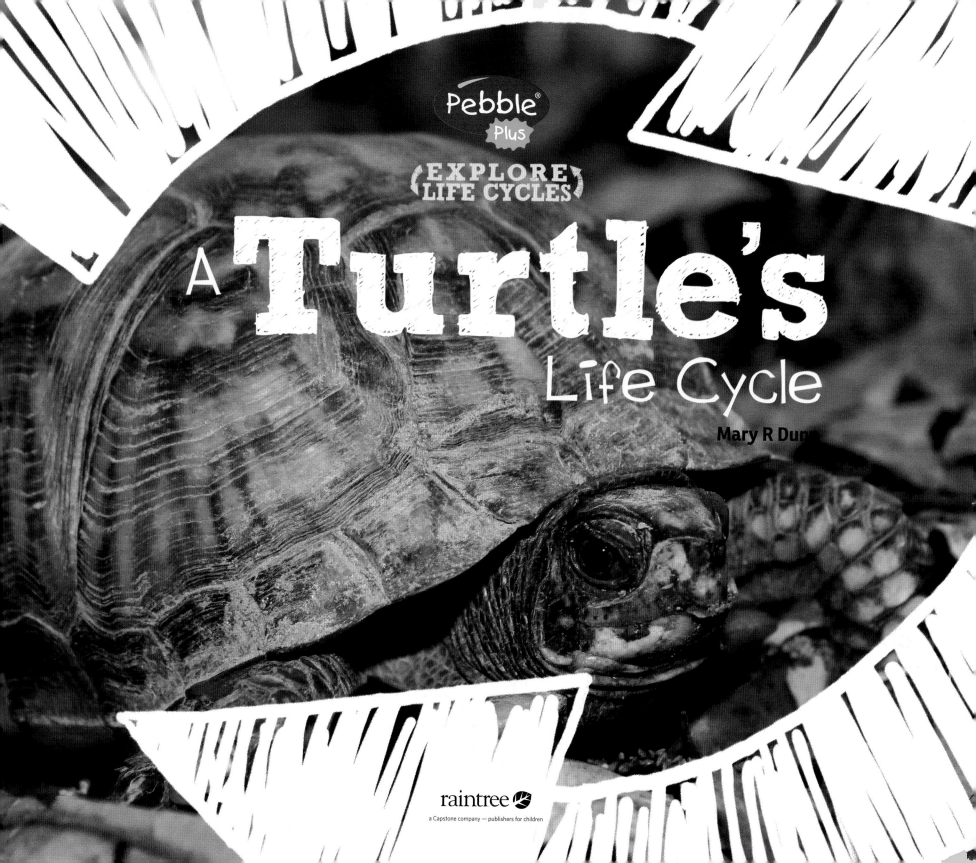

Pebble® Plus

(EXPLORE LIFE CYCLES)

A Turtle's Life Cycle

Mary R Dunn

raintree

a Capstone company — publishers for children

Raintree is an imprint of Capstone Global Library Limited, a company incorporated in England and Wales having its registered office at 264 Banbury Road, Oxford, OX2 7DY – Registered company number: 6695582

www.raintree.co.uk
myorders@raintree.co.uk

Edited by Anna Butzer
Designed by Kyle Grenz
Picture research by Wanda Winch
Production by Kathy McColley
Originated by Capstone Global Library Ltd
Printed and bound in China

ISBN 978 1 4747 4331 0
21 20 19 18 17
10 9 8 7 6 5 4 3 2 1

British Library Cataloguing in Publication Data
A full catalogue record for this book is available from the British Library.

Acknowledgements
We would like to thank the following for permission to reproduce photographs: Alamy Stock Photo: H. Mark Weidman Photography, 21, Robert Hamilton, 13; Dreamstime: Ondreicka, cover; Getty Images Inc: David A. Northcott, 15, E.R. Degginger, 9; Minden Pictures: Lynn M. Stone, 11; Shutterstock: Jason Patrick Ross, 1, KatarinaF, turtle silhouettes, Martha Marks, 7, outdoorsports44, back cover, Ryan M. Boulton, 17, 19, ULKASTUDIO, 5

Every effort has been made to contact copyright holders of material reproduced in this book. Any omissions will be rectified in subsequent printings if notice is given to the publisher.

All the internet addresses (URLs) given in this book were valid at the time of going to press. However, due to the dynamic nature of the internet, some addresses may have changed, or sites may have changed or ceased to exist since publication. While the author and publisher regret any inconvenience this may cause readers, no responsibility for any such changes can be accepted by either the author or the publisher.

Contents

Turtle eggs

A box turtle climbs a rock and slides into a pond. Splash! Turtles are reptiles. Shells cover their backs and bellies.

Box turtles live in woodlands
and meadows. Females need
sandy soil for a nest.
They dig for many hours to make
a nest for their eggs.

Females lay six to eight eggs.

They cover their eggs with soil.

Soil keeps the eggs warm and

wet until they hatch.

Hatchlings

In about three months, the turtles hatch. Hatchlings have an egg tooth on their beaks. They use it to break their shells open.

11

Hatchlings can take two or three days to break their shells.

Some hatchlings stay in the nest.

Others crawl away to see the world.

Young turtles

Hungry young turtles eat during the day. They like worms and slugs. Turtles do not have teeth. They crunch snails and insects with their jaws.

In cold weather, turtles cannot find food. They stop eating and their hearts slow down. Many turtles hibernate underground for the winter.

Adult turtles

Adult box turtles can grow to be 10 to 15 centimetres (4 to 6 inches) long. Many box turtles live to be 50 years old.

Male turtles fertilize the eggs.

Females look for a safe place

to lay their eggs.

The life cycle starts again.

21

GLOSSARY

beak hard front part of a turtle's mouth

egg tooth sharp bump on top of an animal's nose or beak, used to break out of an egg

fertilize join an egg of a female with a sperm of a male to produce young

hatch break out of an egg

hatchling young animal that has just come out of its egg

hibernate spend winter in a deep sleep; animals hibernate to survive low temperatures and lack of food

insect small animal with a hard outer shell, six legs, three body sections and two antennae

meadow big, usually low area of land that is mostly covered with grass

reptile cold-blooded animal that breathes air and has a backbone; most reptiles have scales

woodlands land covered with trees and bushes

FIND OUT MORE

BOOKS

Lifecycles (Ways into Science), Peter Riley (Franklin Watts, 2016)

Turtles, Laura Marsh (National Geographic, 2016)

WEBSITES

www.dkfindout.com/uk/animals-and-nature/reptiles/
tortoises-and-turtles
Learn more about turtles on this website.

COMPREHENSION QUESTIONS

1. Why do females cover their eggs with soil?

2. How do turtles know when it is time to hibernate?

3. In the glossary, find a word that tells what turtles like to eat.

INDEX